15 Ways to Improve Your Reality

Kyla D. Pruitt

Rain Publishing, LLC

Knightdale, North Carolina

Copyright © 2015 by **Kyla D. Pruitt**

All rights reserved. No part of this publication may be reproduced, distributed or transmitted in any form or by any means, without prior written permission.

Kyla D. Pruitt/Rain Publishing
PO Box 702
Knightdale, NC 27545
www.rainpublishing.com

Edited by Rain Publishing

15 Ways to Improve Your Reality/ Kyla D. Pruitt. -- 1st ed.

ISBN 978-0-9962421-3-4

Library of Congress Control Number: 2015940898

Dedications and Acknowledgments

I think Dedications are designed for those who have inspired me along the way. I've had many obstacles that have not only prepared me for this journey, but that have also motivated me to keep moving!

To Big Ma - Look, it's here! She's gone home now, but she was my life. Almost everything I've accomplished is because she dropped soul nuggets along the way. She inspired me to keep pressing, and told me I could and better do it! Words can't describe the pain I feel losing her, but I'll always cherish our moments, talks, wisdom and laughs! She was an amazing woman, and now she's an amazing spirit that I'll carry with me until the end of my time.

To my parents - Those three are my best friends. My world, my rock, and my solid ground. God gave me the perfect package.

Ma- you're insane in the best way. You were rough, but I'm so glad you were. You've created a drive in me that can't be erased. I thank you for paving the way and embracing me for me. We've journeyed together through ups and downs, but I wouldn't trade you for the world! I'm so thankful for what we have. I wouldn't be here without you and your sacrifices. We've become total buddies and I'm proud to call you my one and only Mother! There aren't words for the place you hold to me, but I love you and I'm so excited to go through this journey with you.

Mommy - you know you're my lady! You have to be one of the most selfless ladies in the world. You've taught me what it's all about. Our bond is unbreakable and I wouldn't be where I am today without you. God knew what I needed and in you He gave me the perfect combination. You're my heart - we're knit together and you're my BF! I love being your ONLY daughter. So glad I don't have to share.

Dad - you're literally the piece that holds me together. All my life, you've been my biggest fan, my encourager, supporter, and you told me I could do anything! You've helped me set my dreams in place and helped me go after them in every way. I'm amazed that one person can love someone so much! I understand love because of you. Even though most days you don't take me seriously - you're EVERYTHING to me. I love and thank you!

To my kids - you two are mommy's greatest accomplishments. One day, you'll read this and understand that everything I've ever done has been for you two. You two have single-handedly made me the happiest woman alive and knowing I get to raise such awesomeness is enough for me. If I did nothing else but watch you two grow - that would be enough. I love you!

To my covenant family and friends - what can I say, other than "How on earth did you do it?" "How have you managed all this time with me?" I tell you all how I feel on a regular - but, I must say to the world, I thank God for each and every one of you! I can't name everyone, because there are many that have supported me, however; these people have seen me at my worst and my high points, through season changes, and life cycles. Thank you for everything! This journey wouldn't be complete without you.

A special thank you goes to my Pastors Michael and Connie Smith, Elders David and Cynthia Goodin, Elders Derrick and Zelphia Raines, The McCaskill Family, The Hansen Family, The Hawkins Family, The Harris Family, The Jackson Family, The Joyner Family, The Wooten Family, The Grafton Family, Ms. Chapman, Ms. Wilson, Ms. Poole, Ms. Penn, Ms. Wright, and my entire CJAX family and personal support system!

CONTENTS

Introduction

Gossip 1

Lying 5

Loneliness 9

Being a Workaholic 17

Insecurity 19

Late Nights 21

Relaxation 25

Criticalness 27

Time Management Skills 31

Motivation 35

Building Lasting Relationships 41

Taming Your Emotions 47

Bitterness 51

Giving Back 55

Success 59

ABOUT THE AUTHOR

Introduction

Being a woman is a skill that requires great wisdom. I believe we were created to change lives and go above and beyond to achieve results at such a high altitude that others can't comprehend. Women are branded and built to be crafty.

In this book you will find many topics to help you not only be a better you, but to overcome and disassociate yourself with negative behaviors. You can anticipate identifying yourself in many of these categories, but by the end of the book you will find that you've not only accomplished identifying an authentic you, but you will have grown into a successful and fully functional REAL woman.

Time and time again, I think all women struggle with WHO they are and what they are to do. This is because a woman fills many roles in the lives of many. We are mothers, wives, daughters, role models, the help, house cleaners, cooks, and more. This is not to say that there aren't men who play some of those roles, but a man's primary role is the provider. Even so, a man's first love, example, and perceived reality comes from a woman. In light of this truth, it would seem that men and women would have an easier time relating to one another, but that is often not the case. I believe that men can have better interactions with women when the woman is whole and complete.

This book will help you find your wholeness and completeness by leading you back to your purpose. When I say purpose, I don't mean what you are to do in life, I mean what you were before "the stuff" entered into your life. We all came into the world in the purest form and were innocent until life got a hold of us. Just know that "the stuff" is NOT who you are, but rather things or incidents that have happened to you. None of it defines you, not your past, not your situation, not your material goods, but your heart. That is what and who you are. Remember that!

DISCLAIMER: By no means is this book designed to conflict with your spirituality or what you believe in. My desire is to show you or at least explain from my perspective WHO you are as a woman. No matter what your belief system is, this book is a good starting point to recreate the new you! Change your mindset and enhance your reality.

Proverbs 31:10-31 New Living Translation (NLT)

A Wife of Noble Character

Who can find a virtuous and capable wife?

>She is more precious than rubies.

Her husband can trust her,

>and she will greatly enrich his life.

She brings him good, not harm,

>all the days of her life.

She finds wool and flax

>and busily spins it.

She is like a merchant's ship,

>bringing her food from afar.

She gets up before dawn to prepare breakfast for her household

>and plan the day's work for her servant girls.

She goes to inspect a field and buys it;

>with her earnings she plants a vineyard.

She is energetic and strong,

    a hard worker.

She makes sure her dealings are profitable;

    her lamp burns late into the night.

Her hands are busy spinning thread,

    her fingers twisting fiber.

She extends a helping hand to the poor

    and opens her arms to the needy.

She has no fear of winter for her household,

    for everyone has warm[b] clothes.

She makes her own bedspreads.

    She dresses in fine linen and purple gowns.

Her husband is well known at the city gates,

    where he sits with the other civic leaders.

She makes belted linen garments

    and sashes to sell to the merchants.

She is clothed with strength and dignity,

    and she laughs without fear of the future.

When she speaks, her words are wise,

and she gives instructions with kindness.

27 She carefully watches everything in her household

and suffers nothing from laziness.

Her children stand and bless her.

Her husband praises her:

"There are many virtuous and capable women in the world,

but you surpass them all!"

Charm is deceptive, and beauty does not last;

but a woman who fears the LORD will be greatly praised.

Reward her for all she has done.

Let her deeds publicly declare her praise.

1

Gossip

Gossip comes first because it is a silent killer to ladies. It produces and reproduces hatred at a toxic level. I have often wondered about the purpose of gossiping. I am not saying I'm perfect, nor am I saying I have never gossiped. What I am saying about gossip is that I have watched tremendous relationships suffer and many lives fall to pieces because of it. I imagine that when one gossips they don't believe it's gossip, so let's define it. According to Merriam – Webster, gossip by definition is when a person habitually reveals personal or sensational facts about others or a rumor or report of an intimate nature. Often, words or subjects are discussed among each other and believed to be true.

When you gossip you are dishonoring yourself and performing a disservice to the other person because you prove to be an excessive talker about topics unrelated to you. The best way to overcome and avoid gossip is to remove yourself from the arena. Don't leave the door open to converse about something or someone, especially if it has nothing to do with you. The last thing you want is to be associated with a conversation that was in some form negative. You'll find yourself being reactive as opposed to proactive.

When it comes to conversing with your friends, you should always keep in mind what could happen or how what was said would be perceived by the person you are discussing. Would that individual be okay with everything that is being said? If not, then it is wise to remove yourself and save that conversation. You could possibly have it with the person you are discussing. Try to catch yourself, even if you are in mid-sentence. This will help you discipline your tongue and mind to keep intimate conversation where it belongs, which is with the person who is the topic of discussion.

Quick Note - You will know when your talk has turned to gossip when you're more interested in the outcome or enjoyment of hearing one's life conveyed in a negative manner. Venting takes place when it reflects back on how you can be better, not how the other person isn't better.

I have discovered that when one gossips with others, subconsciously you are displaying your character flaws, especially in the judgment area. This mean you are partaking in what will begin a vicious cycle that will come back to bite you in the end. What you must realize is that when situations arise in any given relationship, you project your inner feelings onto the other person you are conflicting with. If you are a person who feels people are being sneaky or conversing about you, or when you see them you perceive they have spoken ill of you, stop and ask yourself why? Why do you feel this way? Have you sown seeds of gossip? It is likely that because you have behaved that way in past, you subconsciously don't trust others to NOT DO the same to you. Be mindful! When you attack others, you are attacking yourself.

2

Lying

What is a lie? This appears to be a black and white topic; you are either telling the truth or you're lying. This is correct in most contexts, but is not the main theme of this topic. The issue I want to address is, what happens when you stretch the truth to benefit yourself? What happens when in your mind you have convinced yourself that your lie is exactly how it happened? Either way, it is a lie.

We as women, believe it or not, do this often. Unless you are conscious and aware of this concept, you lie. We lie. We stretch the truth, we conceive and perceive alternate realties, and we assume and are empowered by utilizing crafty words. Lying gives a false sense of power - it gives us the ability to create an outcome that we're happy with and can control. Women like to be in control.

Everyone knows what a lie is, it's the opposite of the truth. But, actually a lie is bigger than that. It depends on who you're lying to. We lie to our friends to gain sympathy, to get them on our bandwagon, to make ourselves more important than we are. We lie to men - to modify our existence, to seem more wholesome, or to indirectly excuse vulnerability.

Sometimes a lie comes from a place of fear, a misconception, or a false reality. Sometimes the lie is told because it simply feels good and helps us avoid something that we are hiding. However, ask yourself if it were you, or if it were someone close to you telling the lie, how would you feel? Being able to see through a lie requires you to see yourself past the consequences. By that I mean, not being able to lie to yourself, as mentioned earlier. For example, if you are lying to a friend to gain sympathy, ask yourself, why do you feel that person wouldn't believe or respect the truth? If you are lying for attention, what is it in you as an individual that feels so ignored that the only way to gain attention is to fabricate a situation or circumstance? These examples are meant to help you uncover the truth behind the lies; peeling back the reasons for not conveying the truth will benefit you. Ultimately, you want to teach those around you that you are a person of integrity, character, and dignity and that is how you will react at all times. Note: No lie is a simple lie, it all indicates something significant. Whether it means something to you for lying about the situation or if it meant something to you to lie to that other person, it indeed means something. You must discover what the lie means to you and if it is worth the price you will ultimately pay.

Here's the truth behind lying - it is a direct reflection of your insecurities. It is as simple as understanding that you're not content or happy with any given situation and to fill a space - you lie. This ladies, is a false reality. It tricks you into thinking you're someone you're not. Unfortunately, the ugly truth is that when you lie, you don't like yourself or the person you're lying to. I can advise you that living and being caught in a lie will always be worse than simply telling the truth. You can't change the past - but you can adjust your future. Start making conscious decisions to evaluate your root holes instead of filling them with more junk! Evaluate yourself at this time and right your wrongs. You'll find yourself lifted instead of weighted down.

Once you have committed to being truthful, you will not only begin to be truthful with others, but with yourself too. Lying starts with self because in order to do so, you must first desire and create self-indulgence and gratification. You know when you are planning to be dishonest. As you get ready to do that, ask yourself what is the point of it, then ask yourself, what it will solve. At first, it may be a foreign concept to ask yourself why you are lying before the lie is being told. Often, that is a question asked after the lie has been told. However, this will help you address WHY it is you're actually considering lying and will help you process truth. It may be tough at first, but overall, you will thank yourself later for walking upright with the truth.

3

Loneliness

How often do you find yourself lonely? What exactly is loneliness to begin with? I know firsthand what loneliness is and exactly what it can do. It can be such a strong emotion that it overwhelms you and you fall susceptible to poor choices and inappropriate behavior. As a human, we desire connection. We strive for relationships and seek some form of companionship and interaction with both genders. Contrary to what we as people believe, loneliness is not a void that another person or object can fulfill. Loneliness must be fulfilled within.

It is a discovery process of deep self-evaluation. One must examine the depth of the emotion to discover where it derives from. When I first discovered what loneliness actually felt like, I was in awe at its pull. Often, it occurs or is displayed as a result of a situation but, that situation is not a direct reflection of why a person is lonely. Being lonely, for the most part can be exhibited through many smaller unjustified symptoms such as: sex, drugs, work, money, task lists, and even food. This is not an all-encompassing list, but it includes the most common things people display.

In order to address this, a person has to discover self. Discovering yourself leads to filling the void of emptiness that essentially caused the emotion of loneliness. As a person, we become lonely at different moments in our lives. Sometimes we feel like we have it all, but we're at our lowest of lows when we're lonely. People often wonder how they can know so many people, have so many contacts, attend every event, have so much money, but yet suffer from loneliness every day. It is comical that those with the greatest possessions are sometimes the loneliest individuals, and this is often a very hard concept for people outside the major possession bracket to understand. Possessing material goods in my opinion actually increases the amount of loneliness one feels. This is because the more attention one has or attracts, the less genuine the individuals around you become. Loneliness can impact people of all ages, and cultures. It can pertain to individuals with or without children, general and higher educated individuals, married or single persons. No one person or situation is exempt from the feelings of loneliness.

I recommend evaluating your loneliness meter, as we all have one. You need to determine if you are lonely by default or lonely due to a circumstance change. Once you answer that question, ask yourself why? Be aware that it comes in different stages and phases and some of it is healthy and normal. Events such as death of loved ones, moving, graduated kids, divorce, and spousal schedule conflicts are some cases where adjustments have to be made to deal with new feelings. Know that those feelings will soon fade if they are addressed. I am referencing loneliness that causes a lapse in judgment, the items mentioned before: sex, drugs, alcohol, and addiction are areas I call gap fillers. Those behaviors are usually triggered by feelings of lack of support, isolated events, and pity parties etc. You must begin to love yourself and embrace living alone in your own mental space. This opens the door for you to live with and accept someone else into your space.

Find the source of your loneliness by unpacking the isolated and intimate areas of your soul. Deal with those past ghosts, relationships, insecurities and inadequacies. You can do it! In order to truly find the root of loneliness you have to be willing to dig and fight through the locked boxes. If you're filled - help someone else discover how to fill themselves.

4

Being a Workaholic

Why do we throw ourselves into work? When we have problems why is busyness the solution to pass time? We're always told to stay busy and not idle. Why? In essence, this is the worst thing to do. This is because it robs you of the ability to really feel your situation. Here are my thoughts on the deception of being a workaholic.

Typically, when we throw ourselves into anything, but especially work, we are displaying that we have no balance and cannot adjust our mental space. We are unable to adapt to a personal situation, thus making us busy bees. What we are looking for is a place to attach and thrive. This is a high level of dysfunction. We want to seem productive and wear ourselves thin to justify the lack of substance we may feel at the time. Life does not operate on our terms; often we are not allowed to escape or create an ideal situation in order to cope with obstacles that are pressing at that moment. When we approach life in terms of recreating a situation the way we desire it to be, we are alienating ourselves and barely coping with a situation that we may or may not have created. We must realize that just because we are busy it does not mean we're productive. We're actually counterproductive. We expect those in our lives to understand or accept that this is where we are and we have no choice, but truthfully, it is what we've chosen for ourselves.

We must begin confronting issues, and not allow the busyness to take hold and pacify the lack of healthy confrontation that we must attack. What this means is that at some point we all have to settle our lives. Set a schedule and build in rest. Rest is not always a "stay in bed," "lazy day" thing. Rest is defined as preservation. It is the ability to mentally shut down and reflect. Reflection allows perspective. Perspective creates opportunities, and opportunities create wealth - not just concerning our finances. Wealth is the fundamental quality of success by one definition. This is said because wealth is health, support systems, an intact family, lack of struggle to make ends meet etc.

Appreciate those things that busyness cause you to not appreciate. Create ways to keep busyness out by not allowing it to set in. This especially goes for single parents. Single parents are basically mini superheroes. They are almost everywhere doing everything - it is highly encouraged to build in life for you. It is your job to foster an environment that is healthy for your children, but not all about your children.

Quick bite: To married people, be sure to create life for you two - being busy has destroyed bonds by causing separation and attachment to things instead of each other. You have to make a decision to commit time to each other. Not just time you have, but time that you don't think you have. Purpose family vacations, together vacations, consistent date nights, kid free nights etc. Investing in yourself now will lead to a happier you later on.

5

Insecurity

Before we get into the meat of insecurity, my desire is for you to ask yourself, what are your insecurities? Insecurity is a silent killer to every woman in the world. What do you think about that and why? It is my belief that insecurity destroys more relationships than words. It causes assumptions, mind-fillers, gaps of disparity and much more that unfortunately we as women ignore, deny, shun, or disguise.

As women, this may be the worst area and the thing that truly divides us all. Dealing with others' insecurities is much easier than dealing with your own. It amazes me how much animosity we have towards one another over the major insecurities that we weren't born into. If we unpack these insecurities we will discover they were learned or packed on as time went on. These insecurities are generally areas that everyone else can see, but we fail to see or address. The problem is, many women have no idea how to deal with their life or their insecurities. It is a process, I must say – and dealing with them may be rough. However, not dealing with them is certain to eventually destroy your reality, yourself, and your relationships one by one.

Insecurities have come from lies people told you, or societies' perception of what a women is supposed to be. They derive from issues like acceptance, abandonment, self-seeking pleasures, rejection, childhood issues, and even self-abuse. This is why it is important to realize who you are and what you come with. You must know your strengths and weaknesses and honestly evaluate yourself based upon the truths of your mental capacity and nothing else. Once you have done this and truly know yourself, there is nothing anyone can say or do to disrupt your thoughts. Often, we are so critical or hard on ourselves because we don't want others to call us on our issues. We don't desire to really deal with the truth so we pick areas about ourselves and others and begin to downgrade ourselves area by area. This is a sad reality.

Your insecurities have robbed you of actually being a genuine person in relationships because you can't ever be honest. If you are your worst critic how can you be a critic to someone else? That means, due to your own insecurities you are not able to be completely honest with that friend about how she really looks in that dress because you believe her response to the truth will be like your own. This is a huge issue because it comes from a general idea that it is okay to be dishonest with the other person because you are sure they have been just as dishonest as you are being. It's as though you know that you're not being honest nor are you in a position to be, but you don't want the other person to know that you aren't, and you have convinced yourself that they are just as insecure and dishonest as you are. Sounds complex and complicated right? That's because it is! That is exactly what an insecurity is. It is a bunch of assumptions, imaginations, and conclusions that are drawn together based on everything other than a fact or real life situation.

By nature people are flawed, and often when dealing with insecurities, a person conjures up a notion of how much more insecure or flawed they need to be, so that the other person doesn't notice. Unpack the baggage and clutter from your soul - your life depends on it. It is your decision and you make all the rules and have all the power.

It is as simple as rewriting your story and life. Start with minor issues, how you see yourself in the mirror, how you feel in your outfits, what you think about your hair, skin, nails, etc., This will open the door for honest communication with yourself about your flaws. Once you do that, deeper areas will come out, like, why you may check your significant other's phone, why you don't wear certain types of clothing, why you are loud or quiet in certain settings, etc. We must become honest with ourselves; if we're not honest with ourselves, insecurity will always rear its ugly head.

Being secure is being content with who you are and what you were created to be. It is fulfilling every idea and desire that you may have ever envisioned yourself doing or being. This also by default means that you have accepted the flaws you may or may not be able to change.

6

Late Nights

This by far has to be one of my favorite topics that we will discuss. Let us define what late nights actually include. Besides being unrested for the next day, late nights prevent your ability to shut down. Now, here's a little preview into my world. Take note, I seldom sleep; I have not had a normal sleep pattern since high school when days were rather simple. Once I had my son, and became a mother, full-time worker, and full-time student, sleep went away and late nights became the norm for me. I would stay up all day and night. Sometimes, I would sleep or nap in the day just so I could stay up all night to do nothing more than work. I didn't realize this was a problem until I no longer could adjust my world to day-living. I realized that everything ran together, and at night, my mind went places it should have never gone.

Regardless of your relationship status, late nights build anticipation of the unknown. Working hard late and having frequent late nights are different in some contexts. Now, the occasional late night is typical when your mind wanders. It creates anxiety if you're unfocused and no mission is set in your mind. However, even with direction, late nights turn into discrepancies in life. Most ladies will say they enjoy the nights, dark and silent, and those moments may truly be reflective. However, how many times do late nights turn into isolation, crying spells, a heart-wrenching situation, or worse, sleepless nights? Having frequent late nights sometimes prevents a way for healthy brain digression. The extra stress, the over-compensation, and anxiety, come from neglecting the normal progression of a day.

What needs to happen to avoid these late nights? For starters, more talking. You need to communicate about what you are dealing with on a daily basis - whether it is to your best friend, a journal, a parent, a significant other, anyone, but yourself. When you are not sound, you are tired. When you are unable to process information swiftly, it is because you are tired. The moodiness, anger, emotional battles, over-eating, and insomnia come from the exhaustion in your mind. You don't need sleep, you need a mind break. You need to rest upon rest. At the end of every day, process through it. Get EVERYTHING out! The good, bad, ugly, pretty, etc. After that, do something mindless; laugh, read, cook, drink tea, look online, check a social media site, do something that changes your gears. Then, get ready for bed and lay down. When the night has ended, let it end. Turn over, sleep, and wake up refreshed.

7

Relaxation

Relax? What's that? Who has time? I would be happy just sitting still, but that isn't enough. It is just what we call relaxing. I used to believe that relaxing was getting my hair and nails done, running errands by myself, not answering phone calls or emails. All that sounds like relaxing doesn't it? It does, except it's not truly relaxing. Some think relaxing is pampering, others believe it's idleness. Truthfully, it's what you define it as. However, I believe relaxation is the key to mental stability. When you're tired - your mind is not good at producing great results. This is something I addressed in the "Late Nights" unit. Not relaxing your mind leads to mental exhaustion and a relatively quick burn out. As women, we carry a busy mind by nature. Our mind is always in process improvement mode, but it is important to power down. Do brain-training games, logic games, and shift from task or list mode to enjoyment.

When you are relaxed, you are literally free from all cares, anxiety, and all tension. The funny thing is, you may think you are relaxed, but your body can always tell the difference. How many times have you said, "Man, I feel tense, but I don't know why." Someone may ask, "Well, what's on your mind?" You typically respond by saying, "I don't know, nothing that I can think of." WRONG! You can backtrack and see the connection between the last time you had a good sleep or a mental break to the high levels of anxiety you are experiencing. Even if there is a knot on your back, or a pimple on your face I am also certain that you can trace it back to your lack of relaxation.

Take yourself out! Pamper yourself. Spend time alone, find that one place or thing that really relaxes you and brings you back center, make time for it. Your future self will thank you!

8

Criticalness

Being critical is by far one of the most detrimental qualities a woman can have. It's damaging for anyone and any gender, but in a woman I believe it's worse because it displays a level of inconsistency, as evidenced by being moody, judgmental, and complaining excessively. Sometimes we as people view being critical as an attribute. We run through the fine details, we pick apart every item, and we say, I just made that better. However, that only pertains when a person is actually being constructive. For example, if a person is asked to critique a situation, the other party is open to what they are saying and the other party is receptive to the ideas that are coming at them. Sometimes, even when we are not asked for our input we offer it up. We must ask if we are being constructive and trying to help, or are we just interjecting our opinion to be critical? We know the true answer to that question. Often we use this trait to be overbearing and opinionated. As ladies, we are detailed individuals by nature and we observe everything. We literally scoop out trouble sometimes and we major on the minors. This impacts those around us and is sometimes viewed as "always having something to say," or being extremely talkative. It causes people to tense up and not be themselves because they are overly concerned with the backlash. What we must learn is that people often express and do what they desire when they desire it. It is almost impossible to critique something without criticizing it. If we gain an understanding of the human mind we would realize that sometimes embracing a person's attributes are better than a critique of the individual. When you criticize you vocalize to the person that they are an issue because often you're critiquing something that they've lived with or have been aware of for some time. A person cannot change their makeup - they can only enhance it.

If a person feels as though you always have something critical to say, this violates the trust and authenticity of the relationship. If someone is not asking for a critique, it is usually better to just allow them to be without interjecting your thoughts or opinions. We must learn the difference between a critique and being critical. Being critical is a heart condition in my opinion. It is a form of comparison to the other person to make them look or feel bad, it is a way to throw a dig at a person's hard wiring about themselves. Offering a critique is aiding a person so that they can find a solution. It is collectively coming together to make something better as opposed to leaving that person feeling empty or less-than due to the comments that were made to them.

9

Time Management Skills

For a long time, this page was left blank. I have literally struggled for years to complete this section. Why? Because honestly, time management is developed; it has never been taught in my opinion. You can't teach it because there has to be a sense of urgency about yourself that forces or causes you to manage your time better.

In order to manage your time better you must have something important placing a demand on your time. As a general rule, I was taught that if you're on time, you are late. Be early, not behind. I have discovered a few things after years of being a worker, mother, wife, single, and a servant. One of those are, things happen; the other is, with proper planning, everything can be executed. We say things like, people make time for what they want, or if you would have moved faster, we wouldn't be here. We must realize that when dealing with time we must adjust. Time waits for no one. It moves at a rapid speed and does not care if you have any conflicts. It is extremely unforgiving and very selfish most days. As a woman, in whatever stage you are in, mastering time management skills is so important. Learning how to say no, and when to say no is key.

Now, in dealing with time as a woman, you must strive to always be effective. As a mom, a mistake could be the end of the world to your little person, as a worker, being late costs money. Sometimes time management is the very thing that could make or break any given situation. It is very true that time management requires adjustments that you will fine-tune as circumstances and life phases come and go. A few basic adjustments will enhance life and cause you to see progress if this is a trouble area. Realize that you can't do it all and sometimes you just need help. No matter how much you don't want to ask, push your pride aside, and get assistance if needed.

Look to preserve time and energy if possible. This means, pack at night, lay your clothes out, determine what route to take, etc. This is all about planning and organizing your life. You must find ways to bring ease, because one day you will be requested to do the same for your spouse or children.

Recognize that it is okay to say NO. This seems to be a hard area for women. Don't make an excuse, don't offer a justification. If you can and want to do something, do it. If NOT, simple fix – Don't do it. You are the CEO of your life, you get to decide who you want to hire and fire! Take heed to that simple instruction there. The only thing that should slow you down is your children and even that can be adjusted. Know this, if you are having a hard time in this area that means your priorities are off and planning isn't your thing. That is OKAY. Learn your problem areas and find a way to take dominion over this time issue. Get up early, don't stay out late, make task lists, set reminders etc. Conquering time will empower you in all areas to build a life of timeliness.

Side Note: This will also cause you to depart early for activities too. Mastering time will release you of the obligation of overstaying and arriving on time.

10

Motivation

When it comes to this topic we must ask ourselves, how does one acquire motivation? Is this something we are born with or not? Is this learned? Actually, it is my belief that it is all of the above. As women there is a drive that is in all of us to just make things happen. I believe that motivation along with determination go hand in hand. It is the trait that separates the good from the great and the great from the greatest. Why? This is because everyone is not willing to go the extra mile. This topic actually applies to men, women, and children. At some point we are taught not to give up, not to quit, to keep moving no matter what. Because women bear children and are sometimes considered the underdog, we give this area a lot of weight in our everyday lives. Even when we are fed up, dirt tired, and beyond exhausted we muster up the energy to keep going. It is a very true statement that everyone is not interested in being great or being good. Sometimes that is simply enough. I used to think I would do amazing things in the world – that I would have all the time in the world to do it and I would have fun – until I started doing it. I graduated with a Master's degree at 21. That sounds great – but the price I paid was heavy. It came with long nights, loss of sleep, loss of relationships and a ton of weight gain. At 27, I set out to finish my PH.D and guess what – that too, has been an amazing journey, however, the price has been hefty.

Now, this is not to be looked at from a negative standpoint or that your life will be how mine has been. The purpose of saying all that is to help you understand that motivation, persistence, determination and the ability to keep going has to conquer every area of your life if you're looking to fulfill your dreams and goals. If your desire is to be the greatest by your definition, you'll have to endure some trials and tribulations and you'll have to experience some life changing events. However, if you can stay motivated you can make it through anything. Everything is always alright once time is allowed to do what it does. Time provides clarity and causes perspectives to shift. It attacks real issues and reveals the true source of most inner struggles. When it comes to motivation - we must realize the true beauty behind keeping the fire burning. Stay encouraged.

The negative aspect of this empowering drive is the force that we place on others to have the same level of urgency when it comes to task completion. We sometimes can get beyond frustrated with others and project our way of thinking on the next person and that is detrimental. This is detrimental because we often don't allow people to process or be themselves around us. We are quickly agitated and frustrated when things don't go our way and this can cause a major strain on the ones we love. When we are faced with major personality conflicts, we must pause and consider who we are dealing with. We have to ask the tough questions and allow people to operate in their capacity. Give others a chance to be themselves. Meet them where they are and do not be so swift to alienate or prejudge them because they do things differently. Consider their strengths, weaknesses, and purpose to see how you can grow and learn from that individual. We must check this area within us so that it doesn't push our family and friends away. We should constantly look for ways we can learn from a person instead of acting adversely to the personality clash. I encourage you to breathe.

Determination is something that we all think we have in us, until the time comes to push through. By definition, determination means: a quality that makes you continue trying to do or achieve something that is difficult. Often, we confuse determination with sticking something out when it seems too tough or difficult. In essence, determination is having the ability to maintain a positive mindset and excel beyond a set of negative circumstances.

Sometimes we torture ourselves or force ourselves to stay in uncomfortable situations when we really should walk away. Being determined does not mean you cannot walk away from a task, or strategically quit. Determination simply means you are committed to locating the best possible route for yourself and sticking to that plan. It manifests itself in many different forms. If you slow down long enough to access the drive within you and others, you will see the value in this being a skill, or an art form. This guideline will carry you through many hurdles. Realize that it is okay if something does not get done TODAY, because tomorrow will come. Do not get so bogged down with the task at hand that you alter your perception of what you need to happen and what you want to happen.

Building Lasting Relationships

This is another target area for women, and honestly, people in general. The reason this is a difficult task is because people change. Because people change it takes a certain set of skills to maintain a relationship. A healthy relationship takes work in any context. Building a lasting relationship, through trial and error is an entirely different mountain. One has to be able to compromise, take criticism, believe, and hope the best of the one they love. All of this sounds a little complex, but with hard work and dedication building a lasting relationship can be done by developing skills to enhance your relationship. I will discuss those as you read on. The problem is until an issue arises we are unable to predict what this looks like. We build offenses quickly with those we love based on miniscule situations, not realizing that every day is a learning opportunity. I had to learn this the hard way and have done much damage in relationships before I figured it out. We assume that because someone loves us - they should have our back all the time. What we don't realize is that having your back sometimes means going against you by challenging your objectives, opinions, and even your positions. In maintaining a relationship, both parties are supposed to make each other better. They are to learn from one another, sharpen each other, solve complex issues and poke holes in areas that may not be well thought out. This is for our benefit and protection. There is safety in having good counsel, it saves us from ourselves. We need this because we are not always right.

In relationships - we desire someone to engage us or entertain our dysfunction. Maintaining and having a healthy relationship is far from that. In essence, if we aren't whole within ourselves how exactly can we anticipate any relationship to be healthy, long-lasting and real? It is rather selfish and unfair to anyone to give ourselves in an incomplete or unhealthy state.

Another part of maintaining a healthy relationship is preserving and taking care of ourselves so that we may fully function in a whole capacity for the other person. When we look at being whole, we look at being secure, stable, (mentally and emotionally functional (free from major roadblocks, and able to exchange in an actual friendship. In order to maintain a real friendship we must constantly understand that people change and they do so frequently and sometimes without warrant or justification. Truthfully, an explanation may or may not be owed to you and it may not be explainable at that time. It is not our job to judge a person or even gauge their situation. It is our job to love them without reservation and to understand our differences. Realize that they are not perfect nor should they be. We are to love people where they are, through good and bad and sometimes from a distance. Consider this, sometimes when we are reevaluating relationships we must look from the back seat, and this is okay! It is perfectly normal and healthy to pause. When you have a phenomenal relationship with a person it can be reinvented and has to adjust with the transitions of life. It has to go beyond a surface level relationship and enter into a level of equity. This gives us the ability to know that even when someone is yelling, or saying something hurtful, it doesn't necessarily mean they don't love us and intend to harm us. We must know that even when it looks contrary. Even if it means removing ourselves from a situation to reevaluate the status of the relationship, we ought to know that there is still love there.

If that means parting ways to advance ourselves in life we must know that at some point it will come back around if it ever was a real relationship. As women we strive to understand, we live for details, and generally if we don't understand we are unable to accommodate. This has to change. Understanding a person and loving them are not the same. Of course, this is not to excuse any toxic or dysfunctional relationships. Those are completely separate and must be dealt with quickly and properly before they spill over into a severed, irreparable relationship. This passage is intended to deal only with the normal everyday relationships.

Normal everyday relationships are those that are fulfilling and meeting the needs of both parties. Areas that are thriving in healthy relationships are that of healthy effective communication, respect, love that does not ache, dignity, effective processing of feelings and emotions, etc. They are not selfish relationships where one party's opinions or thoughts are better than the other, or one party is not heard, or there is constant fear. This passage is not meant to deal with toxic and dysfunctional relationships, for example, abuse of any kind, past or present. Those are special cases and must be dealt with from another angle.

If you have a good relationship, try your best to always preserve it and ask yourself if the obstacles you are dealing with can be overcome by simply backing off while still conveying love. Let this encourage you to reevaluate where you have fallen short and give room for error on all sides. Believe me when I say, maintaining healthy, strong relationships are worth it. To know that you have people in your life that will be around for a lifetime, through transitions, life cycles and the woes and joys of life is priceless. You never want to sacrifice your sound relationships.

Taming Your Emotions

Please know this about emotions, they are fickle and change often. Never EVER make a permanent decision based on your emotions. Emotions are very real and have the ability to directly impact everyday situations. Sometimes as women this is our greatest struggle: speaking out of turn and speaking from a place of hurt, rather logic. When we are flustered it is tough to tame or even fully explain what's being felt on the inside. We sometimes say it's hormonal, maybe it is, but often, the emotion streams from a triggered place that offsets a particular set of feelings and we then react as though there is no consequence. One can react in multiple ways; emotions can cause a shutdown, breakdown, breakup, or worse - instability in everyday situations. We must learn to tame this thing we call "emotions." Making any decision quickly, without rationale or logic can cost you years of pain and disappointment. Some examples are when someone has cheated on a significant other because a need wasn't met when they desired it, lying to someone because they didn't want to hear them nag or complain about a decision that was made, or disciplining a child before a parent has received the entire story. Once facts come into play, emotions settle, and logic sets in, a person realizes that there is a better way to handle the situation. Emotions stem from a change that has somehow caused a rapid response but most often does not require a rapid reaction. Notice, I said rapid and require. How often does your situation REQUIRE an immediate response? When we respond in this manner we literally have prohibited our thought process, lost control over an issue, and now have to figure out how to backpedal to fix something that is almost irreversible based on the initial response. Your emotions caused you to imagine a situation or sequence of events that possibly does not exist. How do we know this? Think about what happens when you calm down - you literally reprocess the situation and realize that it was NOT as bad as you thought. You make sense of it - think through the problem, analyze it with clarity and then BOOM - problems and emotions are solved and settled. This is why the "I'm sorry" comes typically within hours of the emotional reaction. When dealing with emotions it is important to stop, breathe, wait, and then respond. Try to walk away or gain understanding before you react. Try to write down your thoughts to dump, then address it.

Here's an exercise - the next time you're angry, write everything down and don't speak. Go back 24-48 hours after the situation occurred and read your feelings. Are they the same? Are they justified? Could you have interpreted the situation the wrong way? These are things to ask yourself when dealing with other people that potentially are conflicted in their thinking too. You will then evaluate the situation and be thankful you did not respond too hastily.

Be encouraged. You may not be able to fix the situation, but you can tailor your response to the emotion.

13

Bitterness

This could be a lengthy chapter, but I won't keep you long. How do you overcome hurt when it leaves you broken in a million pieces, or when you thought someone would never hurt you? I have come up with a simple answer and solution. It is so simple that you may not believe it to be true. What is that answer? It's simple: prayer and forgiveness. The answer is simple, but it may not always be that simple to implement.

Bitterness comes from resentment. It comes from an unjust wrong, so wrong that you carry it with you daily in every situation. It also takes time to heal, but I assure you, in time comes clarity and wisdom and in time you will begin to heal. You will heal by evaluating your role in whatever went wrong. In this thing called time, we learn, we live, we experience hurts, and to prevent those hurts from happening again, we become wise. We transform into new people from every obstacle we face and we recover if we allow ourselves this time.

However, if we become bitter, this changes that process and we stay stuck in someone else's wrongdoing. If we are not careful, bitterness is easily formed from the remnants of anger that have caused significant damage to your soul because you have not yet seen your role in the soul shattering process. You may not be the sole cause of the issues, but you are the sole contributor of your unreleased bitterness.

Ladies, I know this feeling all too well. In dealing with a divorce, physical and sexual abuse, and many disappointments, I learned that life can take a toll on you. Situations and people can leave undealt with emotions, unintended hurts, and unanswered questions altering the fabric of your make up. These issues can cause you to doubt yourself, want to change who you are, and leave you feeling empty.

Letting go of this is no easy task. We lock this area up in a box that we think no longer exists. Inevitably, something happens to trigger our memories of betrayal and we try to deal with it in a way that we ignore the root cause but take out our discomfort on everyone else. How we respond to people derives from this thing called bitterness.

Bitterness creeps into areas that people are sometimes unaware of. It's the reason we're unable to adapt to life, why we cope in unhealthy ways, why we search for love in the wrong places, and usually the cause for a miserable temperament. It's time we check this emotion and begin to heal.

It's important to know that there is nothing you can do to control another person. We sometimes think if we say enough that it will help, but it only deepens the wound that is yet to heal. The result of your bitterness can not be shifted based on another's actions or adjustments. It all starts with a decision to be whole. Then you must be honest with yourself about the flaws you have. Once you accept those flaws and realize who you are, you'll no longer dwell on the source of your bitterness. Accept wholeheartedly the role you played and try not to be that person moving forward. Accept that you can't control people, but you can control yourself.

In controlling yourself, you'll realize that there is nothing wrong with you. If there is, you're in complete control over the change you desire. Fix it! Fix you! Fix your world. There is no reason to walk around with any amount of hatred in your heart because it only hinders the one with the inability to really hate. Truthfully, if you're hurting it is because the capacity to hate is not within you. You were not created to be an angry person, rather a loving person. Reflect on the Proverbs chapter that was included in the introduction to this book, it defines who you are. Start today, by reshaping your life and claiming your healing. Write letters to those who hurt you, and BURN them, Start anew; it is in you and up to you to do so. Trust me when I say, the worst part is over. The actual harm has been done, now move forward. Your future self depends on it!

14

Giving Back

Why do we give back? What does it mean to do so? Often, we give in many areas: finances, time, support, and we often give to the point of exhaustion. However, I've noticed that as people we thrive in this space. We are built to give; it gives us great fulfillment and allows us to feel as though we are contributing to society. There are some people who have formed their life around thoughts like, "I have been hurt or taken advantage of and this will never happen again." Wrong. Truth is, it will happen again, over and over and you must be okay and unphased by this knowing that you have done all you can do. Ceasing to give and walking around in a non-giving mode creates a level of distrust within yourself. You think or often ask yourself how you were in a position to be done so wrong. It was not you, it was them. Now, I am not anywhere near saying, be taken advantage of. This is something we cannot always avoid, nor is this something that we should adjust to.

Unfortunately there will always be people who mistake kindness for weakness. However, you do not have to allow that to shape or mold your perception of others. Yes, you must use better judgment, and yes, you must analyze your weak areas to know how and when to safeguard yourself. Giving lays the foundation for how your life will be governed. Believe it or not, there are many, many, many more people who think like you than not. You will always be in a situation where you will need assistance in this life. Your very creation requires you to be a giver because it makes you selfless. It places a demand on where you are. Think of motherhood. If you are not a mother, think of your mother. Think about how she raised you, or the person who did. We have all been in a place where we have been grateful for help or thankful that favor has been with us in situations

15 WAYS TO IMPROVE YOUR REALITY · 57

that could have been much worse. It is a humbling place to be in any predicament where you can bring ease to the next person without question. If you are stuck in this mode of feeling taken advantage of try to shift your perspective. Attempt to think of this area as an area of foundation for those ahead and behind you. It works! There are simple joys in giving. Give unto to others as you would want them to do for you and yours.

15

Success

What is the definition of success and how do you find your authenticity in your natural giftings? This is an area that is very dear to me. It took me a very long time to accept ME. Because of previous hurts, past mistakes, other perceptions and junk laid on me as I lived life I struggled to actually understand who I was. All of the areas I have discussed have assisted me in the discovery of who I am. As life moves forward, as I have stated before, we all change and we grow. Like you, there are core things about me that may never change. As we continue to grow, our hard-wiring develops and changes. It is so vital to understand exactly who we are. In previous chapters I discussed dealing with your flaws and problem areas, but my heart's desire is for you to embrace who you are to find and locate your authentic self.

As you unpack your problem areas, you must combat those areas with all the good you have in you. You must discover yourself by un-packing all the garbage that has been laid on you. You are a phenomenal women with wonderful qualities. You are all that you desire and dealing with these problem areas will help you fine tune your strengths. This area is designed to now pull all the strong areas out. Think about what you are good at. Write down something every day that you LOVE about yourself and don't hold back. Think about what you are good at. What are your passions? Is it your heart, is it your ability to counsel, to uplift others? Are you a giver by nature? What separates you from everyone else? What would your friends and family say you are great at? Success is what YOU make it. You determine when you feel you have made it. Is it when you have accomplished everything you desired? Is it completing school or making it to a place of stability? Is it that you were the first one in your family to do something? What have you pioneered? Was it your ability to overcome tough situations or circumstances? Think about it! You are great at whatever you put your mind to, but what is it that you have thrived in? Locate that and once you do you are headed into the world of embracing the authentic you. This may not line up with what you or anyone else thought. You may discover that you have been doing things that you really have no desire to do, but did not want to disappoint your loved ones in the process. This is your life, this is your world; you get to live it the way you desire. As long as you maintain your character, dignity and self-respect, you have done nothing wrong! Even though you will find you have changed, embrace that this is the new and improved REAL you!

I hope that through this process of reevaluating your life through this topical read, you will begin to walk this journey to the real you! Embrace change, embrace your growth, and embrace and love you!

ABOUT THE AUTHOR

Kyla D. Pruitt

Kyla Pruitt (born and raised in Joliet, Illinois) is a motivated professional in the legal field (in Jacksonville, Florida). She has a B.S. in Criminal Justice (Florida University, 2008), an M.S. in Corporate Organizational Communication (Northeastern University, 2009), and is currently working on her Ph.D. in Law and Public Policy (2016). The stereotype of a rather humorless, dull, legal professional however, does not apply to Kyla. While she is dedicated to her work and academia. she uses her warmth and compassion together with her astounding knowledge and expertise, not only in her work, but also when fighting for, and advocating for the causes she believes in; both in her personal life as well as in her professional life.

Kyla's work as a Certified Life Coach (2015), as well as her personal life experiences, have made her an understanding, non-judgmental professional, who is able to empathize, as well as find creative, effective solutions to a wide range of personal as well as legal dilemmas. Being a youth leader, mentor, and the mother of two wonderful kids, she is able to understand the difficulties of growing up in different circumstances and the need to have a solid support system. It has been a long, treacherous road to success for Kyla, however her personal experiences as well as her academic triumphs, have made her a source of wisdom, comfort, support and inspiration to many people from various walks of life.

It's Kyla's passion and goal to inspire and empower both men and women of all cultures and backgrounds to build themselves up for their future successes – whether this success is professional, legal, or in their personal lives. Through her legal work, blogs and now her newest accomplishment, a self-help book (15 Ways to Improve Your Reality, Kyla has been able to achieve her personal goals of encouraging growth and development in her community and aims to be an asset on a national level one day to help countless people overcome difficult barriers in their lives.

Some of Kyla's hobbies are going to the beach, getting involved in her community, and creative writing. She is a church leader, and is a passionate debater about the law in regards to laws and policies.

www.ingramcontent.com/pod-product-compliance
Lightning Source LLC
Chambersburg PA
CBHW072105290426
44110CB00014B/1830